Miss Margaret E. Knight &
St George's Field, Sheepscombe

Stuart Eagles

*With a prefatory note by
Elisabeth Skinner*

Published by
The Guild of St George

Illustrations

Front Cover: St George's Field, Sheepscombe (Stuart Eagles, 2014).

p. 3: A map showing the location of St George's Field above Sheepscombe (Land Registry).

p. 5: St George's Field, Sheepscombe (Stuart Eagles, 2014). Inset, lower left and right, the notice boards announcing the meadow to the public (John Iles, 2012 and Kate Gomez, 2015).

p. 7: Knight's Works in Silvertown between the wars (image in the public domain).

p. 8: John Knight's Natural Bouquet Soaps (poster) (image in the public domain).

p. 9: A map showing the modern-day location (marked O, centre) of Avening House (adapted by Stuart Eagles).

p. 10: Agnes Knight, née Underhill (1839-1916), Margaret's mother (Marie Cousens).

p. 11: Nab Cottage, Rydal (image In the public domain).

p. 13: Rapkyns, Broadbridge Heath, Horsham, the Knight family home (Stuart Eagles, 2014).

p. 14: Ada May Knight, Margaret's sister (Marie Cousens).

p. 15: Endways, Margaret's first home in Sheepscombe (Sheepscombe History Society).

p. 17: The original Guild board introducing visitors to St George's Field (courtesy of Cedric Quayle).

p. 20: Greycot, formerly The Cottage, Margaret's home below St George's Field (Stuart Eagles, 2014).

p. 21: Margaret E. Knight (Marie Cousens). Inset, signature from Margaret's last will and testament.

p. 24: M. Barton, Sheepscombe (postcard) (Sheepscombe History Society).

p. 25: A view across Sheepscombe from the edge of St George's Field (Stuart Eagles, 2014).

p. 26: St George's Field, Sheepscombe (John Iles, 2012).

Inside Back Cover: A collage of documents relating to Sheepscombe in the Guild's archives (designed by Stuart Eagles).

Back Cover: St George's Field, Sheepscombe (John Iles, 2012).

For
Cedric and Jim.
Disciples, Companions, Friends.
With thanks.

Acknowledgements

I'd like to express heartfelt thanks to the following people: Elisabeth Skinner for her knowledgeable assistance, support and prefatory note; Sheepscombe History Society, John Iles and especially Marie Cousens for permission to publish photographs; Sheffield Archives, Prof. David Ingram and Dr Cedric Quayle for help with certain matters of research; Dr Sara Atwood and Dr Mark Frost for reading drafts of the text and for encouraging me more generally; Paul Dawson for his invaluable proofreading skills and support; the Master of the Guild of St George, Clive Wilmer, for supporting this publication and Peter Miller for publishing it.

To all those who have helped care for St George's Field, I express a broader gratitude, and single out Cedric Quayle, John Workman, John Iles, Robert Wolstenholme and Kate Gomez, whilst nevertheless acknowledging that it is the people of Sheepscombe themselves, and other visitors to the meadow, who act collectively as its custodians.

I dedicate this booklet to two towering figures in the history of the Guild, both of whom retired as Directors and Trustees in 2014. Dr Cedric Quayle was for many years the Guild's Secretary. His own involvement in the care of St George's Field emerges from the story unfolded here. As Guild Master, Dr Jim Dearden took a particular and keen interest in wildflower meadows. Both have been what Ruskin called 'gentlemen in the best sense' and have been unendingly encouraging and supportive to me personally. This is a small token of my appreciation.

Finally, I thank my parents, who joined me on this journey, both literally and figuratively.

Stuart Eagles
Reading

References in the text to *Works* relate to *The Works of John Ruskin* (39 vols.), ed. E. T. Cook and Alexander Wedderburn (London: George Allen, 1903-1912). *Works* 1.101 refers to volume 1, page 101 etc.

St George's Field, Sheepscombe
A Prefatory Note

On 7 June 2012, the Guild of St George held its Companions' Day in Gloucestershire, visiting Ruskin Mill in Nailsworth and the Guild's wildflower meadow, St George's Field, in nearby Sheepscombe. Local historian, Elisabeth Skinner, provided some significant contextual information about the history of the field, and the identity of its donor.

This beautiful meadow above Sheepscombe was given to the Guild of St George by Margaret Knight, who lived in a small cottage below the Common. People who remembered her thought that she came from the family that made Knight's Castile soap. It is also thought that she was a theosophist. A surprising number of people came to live in Sheepscombe valley in the first three decades of the 20th century, because it attracted theosophists and supporters of the Tolstoyan Colony at neighbouring Whiteway. Both interesting groups of people came to Sheepscombe because of George Jolly, appointed headmaster of the village school situated just below Miss Knight's cottage in 1896. Mr Jolly was a true polymath and a member of the Theosophical Society. He often gave lectures on behalf of the Society in local towns. In the 1920s, two houses further along the lane from Miss Knight's cottage were bought by the Cardiff Lodge of the Theosophical Society as a retreat.[*]

Perhaps Miss Knight came to the retreat and then decided to stay for a while. Certainly Jean Brown of Skippets, who knew her well, said

---

[*] The eminent theosophist, Geoffrey Hodson (1886-1983) described seeing fairies or 'nature spirits' when on holiday with his wife in Sheepscombe Valley. See Sandra Hodson, *Light of the Sanctuary* (1988). Also Florence Tiddeman and her sister, Marianne Spencer, lived here. More generally, the surrounding area is notable for a sympathy to anthroposophy and the legacy of Rudolf Steiner (1861-1925). Ruskin Mill Trust's first educational centre founded on the principles of Steiner, Ruskin, Tolstoy and other progressive educationists, was established at Nailsworth. It might also be observed that nearby villages such as Sapperton were home to leading craftsmen steeped in the ideas and values of Ruskin and Morris, such as Ernest and Sidney Barnsley, Ernest Gimson, Norman Jewson and Emery Walker (SE).

that Miss Knight was a keen theosophist. She also felt certain that Miss Knight had been a nurse in a children's hospital. Indeed, during her time in Sheepscombe, Miss Knight was secretary of the Cranham and Sheepscombe District Nursing Association set up to appoint a district nurse for the villages in 1933.

During the 1920s two bungalows were built on the land below the meadow. Miss Knight must have heard warning bells for she bought the field and gave it to John Ruskin's Guild of St George to save it from development. In later years, three more houses were built on the land below the field, so Miss Knight was right to protect it in this way.

The field was part of an area of land called Rownhams (or sometimes Roundhams) recorded as such as early as 1571. It is possible that it was then part of the woodland, as the document concerns the sale of timber from Rownhams. During the 16th century, Rownhams was inside the deer park that had been hunted throughout the medieval centuries by the Lords of the Manor, whose hunting lodge was at the other end of the valley. By the 17th century, the deer park has gone and a series of hamlets sprang up in the valley which, like many of the Stroud valleys, became a centre of woollen clothmaking. In 1820 the meadow and an adjacent field (now the cricket ground) was divided into plots and cultivated by the people of the village.

Today, every summer, the flowers and butterflies of St George's Field give the people of Sheepscombe great pleasure. Local residents are extremely grateful to Miss Knight, to the Guild of St George and to Natural England for protecting this wonderful meadow.

Elisabeth Skinner

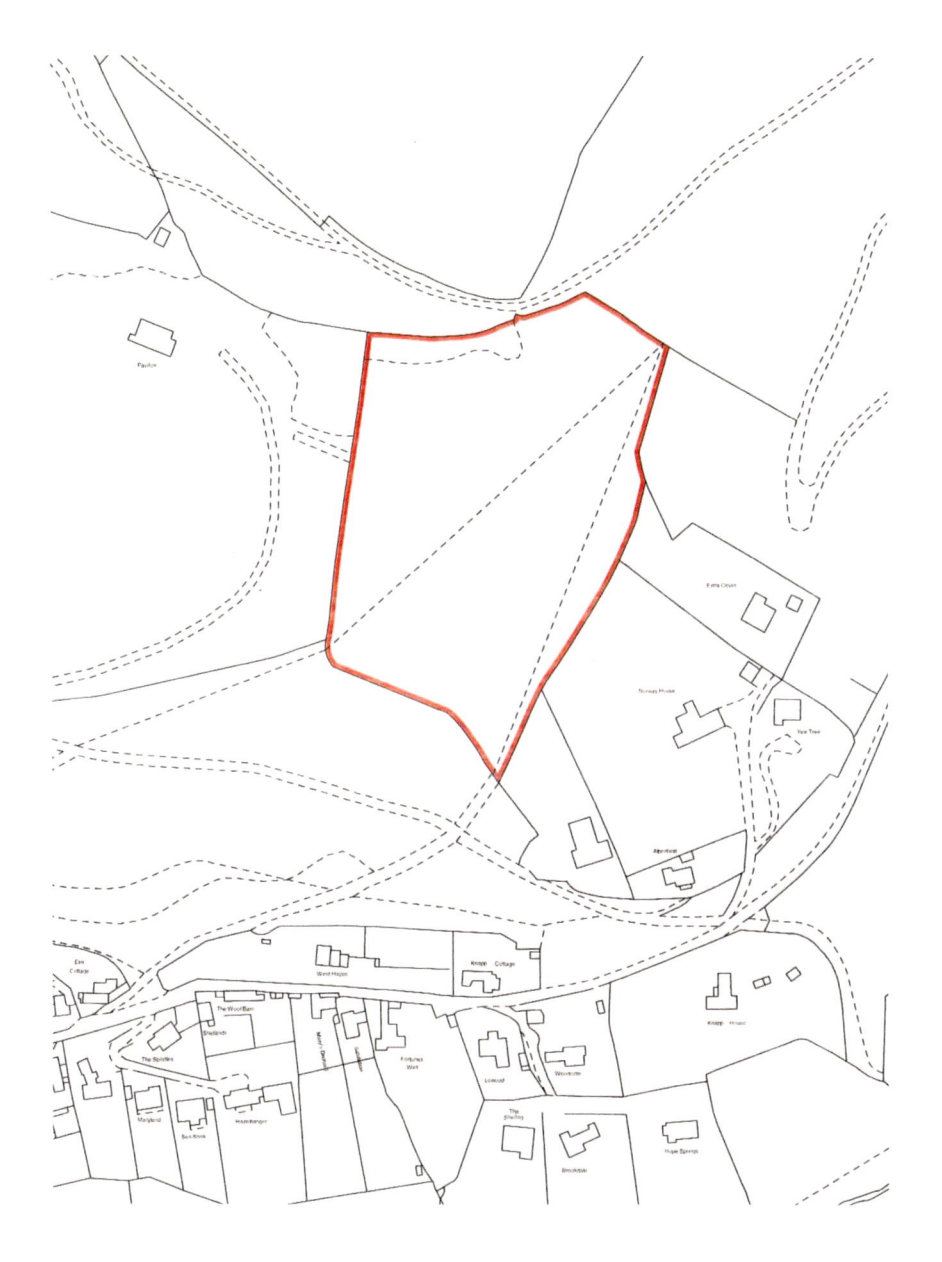

A map showing the location of St George's Field above Sheepscombe.

Introduction

Of all the Guild's donors over the years, 'Miss Margaret E. Knight' has remained one of the most obscure. All I was able to find out several years ago was that her gift to the Guild of a field of 4.8 acres in Sheepscombe, Gloucestershire, was announced in the *Master's Report* for 1936-7. I wanted to know who Miss Knight was and why she gave the Guild a wildflower meadow.

The prefatory note by Elisabeth Skinner of the Sheepscombe Historical Society adds usefully to our understanding of the local context. As someone who has studied in some depth Ruskinian associations with Russia, any link between the Guild and the Theosophical Society, founded among others by the enigmatic Russian occultist, Madame Blavatsky (1831-1891) in New York in 1875, was bound to intrigue me. So, too, any connection with the Tolstoyan colony at neighbouring Whiteway. Could Miss Knight be part of this idealistic, Russian-influenced crowd of theosophists and/or Tolstoyans?

This question provided me with the motivation to investigate Miss Knight more thoroughly. Surely, I thought, someone sufficiently well-heeled as to donate a field to a charity is likely to be the sort of person who left a Will? Not necessarily, perhaps, if she had shared in the Tolstoyans' anarchistic rejection of private property and disdain for legal authority. If I could only find Margaret E. Knight of Sheepscombe in the Probate Calendars, however, it might lead me to relatives, or give by its account of her legacies, an insight into the kind of woman she was. This is to assume that Miss Knight didn't marry. A check of the marriage registers had revealed nothing, but then neither had a check of the death registers! One also had to hope that Miss Knight (it's a common enough name, after all) hadn't moved away from Sheepscombe before she died. Either eventuality might have made it impossible to identify her with any degree of certainty. An electronic search of the indices of Wills had disappointingly revealed nothing. Perhaps she *was* a Tolstoyan after all? Undeterred, however, I embarked on the old-fashioned method of research on which I cut my teeth as a teenage family historian.

St George's Field, Sheepscombe. Inset, lower left and right, the notice boards announcing the meadow to the public.

I read through all the entries for Knight in the Calendars from 1936 onwards. And that's how I found the key that would unlock a chest of research material from which her story can now be told.

That is not to pretend that a complete picture of her life has emerged. I readily admit that some of what follows is necessarily speculative, but most of it is the result of searching family records, census returns, local newspapers and the Guild's archives in Sheffield. Suffice it to say from the outset that researchers have been defeated in the past because, from her earliest days, our subject's name had been subtly altered and it is jolly difficult to find anything out about a person if you don't know her real name. Even if, as is the case here, she neither married nor moved away from the area where one would naturally search for her. Fortunately, the Calendars listed both her real name and her more commonly used alias.

I have not been able to ground Miss Knight's story in Tolstoyan anarchism or in theosophy, but that is only because I have not located any records to that effect. I do not discount the idea that she was sympathetic to either or both. Indeed, I'd like to believe it and hope it's true. The search must go on.

As for the field itself, I can do no better by way of a description than to quote Cedric Quayle in his Secretary's Report to the Board of Directors of the Guild, written after a visit to Sheepscombe in August 1988. St George's Field, he wrote:

> has an extraordinarily rich habitat including 20 species of butterfly. The Small Blue butterfly can be found there and the unusual day-time Burnet Moth. It is a limestone grassland containing a great variety of herbs and grasses largely because for so long it has lain "unimproved" and has been only lightly grazed for a part of each year.

Miss Margaret E. Knight & St George's Field, Sheepscombe

Marguerite Emily Knight was born in the first half of 1870 in the district of St Pancras, London. She was the second daughter of William Duncan Knight (1845-1922) and his wife, Agnes Susannah Frances Underhill (1839-1916). Duncan (as he was known) was a partner in and a director of the family firm of John Knight, the soap manufacturer (remembered for Knight's Castile). The 2 April 1871 census shows that the ten-months-old Margaret (the name-changing had already begun!)[*] resided at 25/26 Fellows Road, Hampstead, situated between today's Swiss Cottage and Chalk Farm tube stations. She lived in the house with her parents, older sister Ada May (1869-1949), a nurse, cook and housemaid. It must have been a comfortable upbringing.

When Duncan's father, William Knight (1819-1910), and William's four brothers, had inherited the soap manufacturing company from their father, John Knight (1792-1864), who had founded the business, they immediately made efforts to expand. When Marguerite was about ten years old, the soapworks relocated from Wapping to the riverside in West Silvertown.

Knight's Works in Silvertown between the wars.

---

[*] Reference to Miss Knight will alternate between Marguerite and Margaret, consistent with the relevant historical record(s) on which that part of the account is based.

By Appointment

Crowned with success
JOHN KNIGHT'S
NATURAL BOUQUET · TOILET SOAPS

Send stamps for 7½d. to Dept. "I.L." for sample box of 6 Special Tablets, POST FREE.

JOHN · KNIGHT · L™   SOAP MAKERS TO H·M·KING·GEORGE·V   LONDON · W

The Royal Primrose Works opened in 1880, named after John Knight's celebrated product that had won a medal at the 1851 Great Exhibition. Marguerite (so styled in the 3 April 1881 census) had moved with her family to Avening House, Arkwright Road, Hampstead, near today's Camden Arts Centre. The family had grown and now included three brothers to Marguerite. On the day of the census a cousin was also living with them and five servants including a cook, housemaids, a parlour-maid and a nurse. By October another brother had been born.

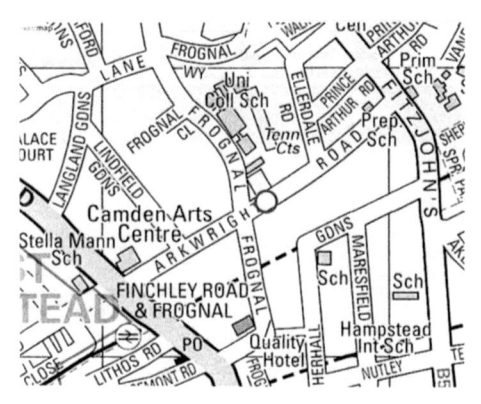

A map showing the modern-day location
(marked O, centre) of Avening House.

    Houses can reveal affiliations, connections and associations that tell us a lot about the family which named them. Avening is a village in Gloucestershire about as far (6 miles or so) south-east of Stroud as Sheepscombe is north-east of it. It was to Avening that Marguerite's maternal grandmother, Sophia Anne Underhill (1809-1850), had moved from her native Oxford in order to restore her health some time after her marriage to Edward Bean Underhill (1813-1901), the Baptist missionary society secretary and writer. Sophia, the daughter of Samuel Collingwood, printer to Oxford University, never recovered, and died when Agnes, the youngest of three children (all daughters) was only ten or eleven years old. That Agnes should later bring up her own children in a house she named after that modest but beautiful Gloucestershire village suggests both an enduring affection for her childhood and a deep love of the mother she lost so prematurely. It also suggests that she possessed a strength of influence as a wife, mother and home-maker, something that apparently though unsurprisingly had a considerable impact on her children. It might well explain how Marguerite came to live in Sheepscombe, so near Avening, many years later.

Agnes Knight, née Underhill (1839-1916), Margaret's mother.

It is not clear how long the Knights lived at Avening House, but by 5 April 1891 (when we next find them recorded on the census) most of the family resided at a house called Stonefield, on what was then Kidbrooke Lane, a country road in Charlton (Duncan and his wife were in fact visiting friends in Bangor, Wales, that night). A visitor to the young Knight siblings was 'Maud B. Worsfield' who is described as an artist. This was actually the portraitist and miniature painter, Maud Beatrice Wors*fold* (1871-1938) whose sister, Edith, went on to marry

Marguerite's brother, William Edward Knight, in 1895. This association with the Worsfolds gives us the merest hint that the family might have taken some interest in art. But much more revealing is where Marguerite herself was living.

The 20-year-old was boarding in Nab Farm or Cottage, Rydal, in the Lake District. Today it is a B&B. It was in this house that the poet, essayist and biographer, Hartley Coleridge (1796-1849), the son of Samuel Taylor Coleridge, had died just over forty years before. Still earlier in the century, Thomas de Quincey had lived there. Ruskin, though by this time largely protected from visitors by his cousin, Joan Severn, was of course living not so far away on the shores of Coniston Water, and we will probably never know if Marguerite ever met him or even glimpsed him there.

Nab Cottage, Rydal.

Marguerite was one of eight young people, all in their twenties, boarding with the farmer, John Armstrong, his wife, Hannah, and their five children. Marguerite was among three people with no listed occupation, but among the other lodgers there was an American, a marine underwriter, and two art students. One of the art students was born in Kew, possibly suggesting a connection with the botanic gardens. For our understanding of Marguerite's later interest in the wildflower meadow at

Sheepscombe, there are two fellow lodgers of particular significance. One, Frederick Ernest Weiss (1865-1953), was a 'demonstrator in [the] botany school' and the other was the recently appointed Quain Professor of Botany at University College, London, Francis Wall Oliver (1864-1931). Weiss had been Oliver's student and was appointed Professor of Botany at Owens College, Manchester the following year, and had become the University's Vice Chancellor by the time of his retirement in 1930. He made Manchester the main centre of botanical teaching and research in the north of England. A distinguished botanist, he was recognised by the award of the Victoria Medal of Honour (VMH) of the Royal Horticultural Society and by election to the Royal Society.

Francis Wall Oliver was the son of Daniel Oliver (1830-1916), the botanist who from 1864 was Keeper of the herbarium and library at the Royal Botanic Gardens, Kew. In *Proserpina, Studies of Wayside Flowers* (1875-86) Ruskin called Daniel 'my botanical friend, good Mr Oliver' (Ruskin, *Works*, 25.331) and Cook and Wedderburn, Ruskin's editors, noted that: '[Ruskin's] obligations, in botanical matters, to Professor Oliver are recorded in *Proserpina* … though that distinguished botanist (himself, too, an amateur artist) regarded Ruskin, I fear, as a quite incorrigible pupil.' (*ibid*, 25.xlvi) Francis became a Fellow of the Royal Society at the age of 41 and was a recipient of the Linnean Medal. Weiss and Oliver were remarkably talented young men whose careers reveal a passion for field botany, the study of flowers in the wild.

We do not know how long Marguerite stayed in Rydal, but her contact there with the botanists uncovered by the census would seem in large part to explain both her association with Ruskin and her passion for wildflowers, of which St George's Field is the enduring legacy.

Marguerite and her sister Ada, neither of whom ever married, probably made their permanent home with their parents until their father's death in 1922. Neither sister, however, was at the new family home of Rapkyns in Guildford Road, Broadbridge Heath, Horsham on census night, 31 March 1901. It is not clear where they were, but Rapkyns, a well-appointed property, would prove to be Duncan's last home. It is now a care-home for fifty disabled and elderly residents, with forty acres of grounds, run by Sussex Health Care. On 2 April 1911, Margaret (now so styled) was visiting her widowed maternal aunt, Sophia Catherine Allen (1837-1929) in Poole, Dorset, accompanied by her parents. But the details of this middle period of her life remain obscure.

Rapkyns, Broadbridge Heath, Horsham, the Knight family home.

One small insight into Margaret's character (and it seems that from this period she was more likely to call herself Margaret than Marguerite) comes courtesy of a letter written in response to another correspondent in *The Times* about a particular theatrical convention.

> Sir.—I should like whole-heartedly to endorse your correspondent's letter in yesterday's issue on the subject of raising and lowering the curtain immediately after each act of a play. I, too, intensely dislike having my enjoyment spoiled and my illusions destroyed in such a rude and abrupt way. When the acting is really good it is especially objectionable.
>
> It is a deplorable custom, and I sincerely hope that there are many others who would like to protest against it.
>
> Yours faithfully,
> M. E. Knight.
> Rapkyns, Horsham.
>
> —*The Times*, 25 March 1922.

Marguerite's brother, Alan Collingwood Knight, had died at Gallipoli in June 1915, and her mother, Agnes, had died in January 1916. Her father, Duncan, passed away on 4 October 1922. Probate was granted to Margaret on 6 December. Her father was worth a considerable fortune: £109,543 15s 2d (about £5m in today's money).

In 1926, Margaret accompanied her sister, Ada, on board a ship bound for Morocco. Ada permanently emigrated there, living in Tetuan as a missionary. At the time of her departure, Margaret was living at Boundary Road, St John's Wood.

Ada May Knight, Margaret's sister.

Now in her mid to late fifties, Margaret moved to Sheepscombe, quite possibly attracted to this part of Gloucestershire by her mother Agnes's early, fond memories of Avening. There is certainly further evidence of the influence of Agnes and Agnes's missionary father, Edward Underhill, on her and Duncan's other children. Not only was Ada a missionary, but her brother, Oliver Hayward Knight (b. 1876) was a member of the Church Missionary Society in Japan.

Margaret was certainly living in Sheepcombe by 1928 when she advertised the sale or exchange of her Austin 7 saloon in the *Gloucester Citizen*. Coincidentally, the local motor-car dealer was Harry Knight (no relation) whose business failure was reported in the papers in 1930. Margaret's intention was to procure a larger motor car and one would like to think that she drove it herself along the steep and stony slopes and narrow lanes of the valleys. Elisabeth Skinner notes that coincidentally Miss Knight contributed to fundraising to buy the vicar a car around this time. For a short while, when she first moved to the village, Miss Knight lived at Endways (on Church Hill and still so-called) but for nearly 20 years and until her death she lived at The Cottage (now Greycot) situated between Church Orchard and Hill House.

Endways, Margaret's first home in Sheepscombe.

We may never know exactly why it was to the Guild that she gifted her field when she was in her mid-sixties. The minutes of the Guild's board of trustees held at Le Play House on 6 November 1936 recorded that:

> The Master explained that an offer of a piece of land at Sheepscombe near Stroud, Gloucestershire, had been made to the guild (sic) by Miss Margaret Knight. The land was about 5

acres in extent and adjoined a common. It was felt that the Trusteeship of pieces of land too small to be taken by the national trust was a very suitable undertaking for the Guild. If someone could be found on the spot to act as the Guild's representative that would be very helpful. There might be some small expense involved over the upkeep of fences, but against this it might be possible to let the land for grazing, which it was hoped would provide enough income for this purpose. The Master said that he and Mr Farquharson were going to Sheepscombe on the following day, and members agreed that if the results of this inspection were satisfactory the Guild would be justified in undertaking the ownership.

—Sheffield Archives: GSG22 box 1, minute book 1928-1952.

T. Edmund Harvey (then Master) and Secretary Alexander Farquharson (who became Harvey's immediate successor) duly visited. The field was officially received by the Guild in the *Master's Report* for 1936/7 in which Harvey wrote:

> Immediately after our last Annual Meeting I visited the Cotswold village of Sheepscombe in company with Mr. Farquharson and discussed with Miss Margaret Knight her generous offer of the gift of five acres of land which she wished to preserve as an open space for the benefit of the people of the village. We made a careful inspection of the land which lies on a hillside immediately above the village and was in danger of being utilised for the creation of unsightly shacks. I am very glad that it has been proved possible to accept the gift of this land, to which free access will thus be given to the villagers. The right of grazing has been let for a small sum to an adjoining farmer and a well-made oak notice board has been placed by the entrance, with the following inscription cut in it:
>
> GUILD OF ST GEORGE
> This field is held for the enjoyment of the people of Sheepscombe.

Please help to keep in order and leave wild plants, birds, and animals undisturbed.
—*Master's Report* 1936-7, p. 6
(thanks to Cedric Quayle for this record).

The original board.

Land Registry records show that the conveyance, made out between the Guild, the Stroud Building Society and Douglas Frederick West was completed on 22 January 1937 and Miss Knight signed the Roll of Companions later that year. There can be no doubt that Professors Weiss, Oliver and Ruskin would have appreciated saving rural land from unsympathetic development and encouraging the growth of wildflowers.

Cedric Quayle, writing in the Guild's newsletter, *Fors* in November 1994, noted that, 'Over the years it has been lightly grazed with no chemical fertilizers ever being given. The result is a limestone grassland with an extraordinarily rich habitat of herbs, grasses and butterflies and of great interest...' (See 'The Guild's Field at Sheepscombe' in *Fors* (November 1994), pp 20-21, quote p. 20).

A report in 1942 noted the following:

> The grazing rights of the Guild's land at Sheepscombe continue to be let to a tenant, the public enjoying full right of access to the land. Owing to war conditions the carved oaken notice board, whose wanton destruction I reported last year has not been replaced. I am glad to say that a local advisory group has been formed consisting of Miss. M. E. Knight, Mr. A. C. Browne and Mr. George Sollars.
>
> —Sheffield Archives 1991/55 add no. 136
> 'Sundry Correspondence 1929-1947'.

Probably the first person to rent the field for grazing was Miss Jean Brown of Skippets. In the years 1941 and 1942, she paid 35 shillings per annum, an amount of rent she had proposed and which the Guild had accepted. In her early letters to the Guild she had written that she felt it was a pity that the grass was not being used for animal feed in war-time, when few of the villagers were going there for picnics. She did make an attempt to purchase the field through her agent at J. Pearce Pope and Sons, Gloucester. In a letter dated 21 November 1941, Will Pope wrote:

> While quite appreciating the good your Guild has done, and is doing, it did occur to me that in purchasing a field in such a small village as Sheepscombe, practically adjoining the Common, was not quite as necessary as in other parts.
>
> —Sheffield Archives 1991-55 add no. 29,
> 'Correspondence 1929-1947'.

He went on to suggest that from the proceeds of the sale the Guild might 'invest ... in other properties in a more needed district'. Mr Farquharson did not correct the misunderstanding about how the Guild came to own the land, but on behalf of the Master curtly informed Messrs Pope that the Guild was 'not considering' such a sale (3 December 1941).

The Guild's archives contain a letter dated 15 September 1943 to a Mr Sidney Hogg which refers to a letter from Miss Knight relating that she had received an enquiry from Mr Hogg asking for shooting rights over the field. The letter goes on to say that the Master 'thinks that the field should be, as far as possible, a sanctuary for wild life and that no permission for shooting should be given unless in some exceptional case to protect other birds or crops. You will, I am sure, understand that protection of wild life is a matter in which the Master and members of the Guild are closely interested.' (Sheffield Archives 1991/55 add no. 136 'Sundry Correspondence 1929-1947') Arthur Browne, a local farmer, succeeded Miss Jean Brown in renting the field. George Sollars, builder and contractor, in a note dated November 1943, wrote: 'I have recent[ly] had conversations with Miss Knight and Mr Brown (*sic*) who is renting the [field]. I have suggested that Mr Brown (*sic*) undertake to make the fence safe for his cattle at his own expense and that he be allowed a period rent-free to pay for such work[,] the cost of which I put roughly at Ten Pounds[. I]f this arrangement be acceptable to you I will on hearing your confirmation arrange with Miss Knight for this to be done.' (Sheffield Archives: 1991/55 add no.29, 'General Correspondence 1929-1947'.) How long this advisory group remained in place is unclear, but it is likely that the Guild responded positively to such guidance as it provided.

Margaret Knight died on 15 February 1949, aged 78. Probate was granted on 14 April to the family solicitor and a cousin, the Rev. Cecil Bertie Howard Knight of Hutton Rectory, Brentwood, Essex. Her estate was valued at £8267 9s (approximately a quarter of a million pounds today). She left £4000 in trust for life to her friend, Suzanne Grahame Hoyer (1877-1966), who had lived with her since at least the 1920s; outbound ship passenger lists show that both women had at one time lived in Boundary Road and that Suzanne accompanied Ada and Margaret to Morocco in 1926. Margaret's last will and testament, made in 1946, included many £50 legacies for her nephews. Property inherited from her father, probably Rapkyns, she left, together with some other personal effects, to her sister, Ada. Margaret directed that her body should be cremated, at a time when less than 5% of funerals were cremations, though the choice was favoured by theosophists. It seems likely that there is no memorial stone or plaque to commemorate her life, and certainly none has been located.

Greycot, formerly The Cottage (left-most),
Margaret's home below St George's Field.

Ada May Knight survived her sister by little more than a month and died in Morocco on 18 March 1949. Probate records record she had formerly lived at The Cottage, Sheepscombe, although this claim might have been a mere legal formality. Her estate was valued at £9560.

In the years immediately after Margaret's death, the Guild seemed less interested in the Field, and certainly less engaged with its management. The slope on which it lies and the lack of a water supply, had defeated attempts to utilise it for practical community purposes. In 1952/53, the grazing' rights were assigned to Mr Finch, of Flock Mill Farm. In 1960, the Master and Secretary of the Guild visited Sheepscombe and met Mr Finch, who agreed to lease the field on a continuing basis, an arrangement that lasted until he moved away from the area.

Margaret E. Knight

From the late 1950s to the late 1980s, the Guild benefited hugely from the advice, expertise, care and conservation management of the late John Workman OBE, owner of the Ebworth Estate and Forestry Adviser to the National Trust. In a letter to Cedric Quayle, the Guild's Secretary, dated 22nd August 1988, he wrote of this 'lovely little field' and the importance of 'keep[ing] the field as it is and as it has been probably for centuries.'

In 1971, the field was designated a site of special scientific interest (SSSI) in the Cotswolds by the Nature Conservancy Council (the forerunner of today's Natural England). In 1972, the Guild leased the field to the Gloucestershire Trust for Nature Conservation at a yearly rent of £10. And on 6 October 1994, St George's Field became a part of the Cotswold Commons and Beechwoods National Nature Reserve.

In marking that occasion, Janet Barber, a council member for English Nature, remarked: 'While the field, and its surrounds, look very attractive this morning, (there is flowering marjoram and hairbell), it of course comes truly into its own in early and mid-summer with a lovely variety of flowering plants, many very rare, including orchids, vetches, flax, and cowslips with attendant interesting butterflies.' (qtd. in Quayle, *op. cit.*, p. 21).

The Guild can be proud that, together with Natural England, it so carefully preserves what is surely Miss Knight's greatest legacy. To appreciate this beautiful wildflower meadow in Gloucestershire is to have learned one of Ruskin's most important lessons. 'I suppose,' Ruskin wrote of himself in 1876:

> few men now living have so earnestly felt—none certainly have so earnestly declared—that the beauty of nature is the blessedest and most necessary of lessons for men; and that all other efforts in education are futile till you have taught your people to love fields, birds, and flowers. Come then, my benevolent friends, join with me in that teaching.
>
> —*Works* 34.142

Margaret Knight probably knew that passage personally. Ruskin wrote it in support of the protest against the incursion of locomotives deeper into the Lake District. That successful campaign was led by Robert Somervell (1851-1933), like Miss Knight, a member of a prominent manufacturing family (his father founded K Shoes of Kendal).

One of the earliest Companions of the Guild of St George, and probably its first Secretary, Somervell was resisting a perceived threat to extend the railway line from Windermere to Ambleside and Keswick, via Rydal. Miss Knight might well have drawn some inspiration from that. After all, it was at Nab Cottage that she lived with the young botanists, Professors Weiss and Oliver. It was at this same property that Somervell had spent one Sunday afternoon in 1874/5 with the social reformers, Octavia Hill (1838-1912) and her sister Miranda (1836-1910). 'I walked over to Rydal, to Nab Cottage,' Somervell wrote:

> and spent hours of delightful talk, in which, with many other things, I heard the story of [Octavia's] rent-collecting work in London, which Ruskin had given her the chance of starting by buying, and placing in her care, two tenement houses.
>
> — *Robert Somervell, For Thirty-Three Years Assistant Master and Bursar of Harrow School: Chapters of Autobiography*,
> 'edited with additional material by his sons'
> (London: Faber and Faber, undated) p. 59.

In saving 'some small piece of English ground, beautiful, peaceful, and fruitful' (*Works* 27.96) as Ruskin hoped Guildsmen and women would do, and in offering it to the care of the Guild nearly eighty years ago, Margaret E. Knight of Sheepscombe became a true disciple of Ruskin, and a Companion to whom we should all be grateful.

Stuart Eagles is Secretary of the Guild of St George, and the author of After Ruskin: The Social and Political Legacies of a Victorian Prophet, 1870-1920 *(Oxford University Press, 2011).*

Sheepscombe.

(*Left*) St George's Field can be seen in the top right hand corner.
Margaret Knight's home, The Cottage, is in the centre of the picture. The wall that crosses horizontally through the centre of the picture is the road called Far End Lane. There are three groups of cottages around the wall.
The Cottage is in the middle group on the left and above the road.
The photograph is from the early twentieth century.
(With thanks to Sheepscombe History Society)

Looking across Sheepscombe from the edge of St George's Field.

St George's Field, Sheepscombe. An 'extraordinarily rich habitat' attracting many species of butterfly.

Ruskin Lectures

Original Series
1978   Lord Asa Briggs
1979   Robert Hewison: Art & Society. Ruskin in Sheffield in 1876
1981   Philip Rawson: Ruskin, Turner and Time
1982   Van Akin Burd: Ruskin, Lady Mount Temple and the Spiritualists
1982   Michael Kitson: Ruskin's 'Stones of Venice'
1983   Joe Holyoak: J. H. Chamberlain. Ruskin's architect of the Civic Gospel
1985   Anthony Harris: Why do our little girls have large shoes?
1986   Tim Hilton: Ruskin's Masterpiece
1987   Sir Roy Shaw: The Relevance of Ruskin
1988   Nicholas Shrimpton: Ruskin and 'War'
1991   Anthony Harris: Ruskin and Siena
1992   Malcolm Cole: Be like Daisies
1994   Royal W. Leith III: Ruskin and his American followers in Tuscany

New Series
2005   Stephen Wildman: Thomas Matthews Rooke
2006   Sam Smiles: Ruskin and Cambridge
2007   Jacqueline Yallop: Our Power to Bequeath
2008   Paul Tucker: Charles Fairfax Murray and Duccio's *Maesta*
2009   Robert Hewison: Of Ruskin's Gardens
2010   Stuart Eagles: Ruskin and Tolstoy
2011   Zoe Bennett: The True Use of Faith
2012   Howard Hull: Demeter's Dowry: Ruskin and Landscape
2013   Mark Frost: Curator and Curatress
2014   Gray Brechin: "Necessitous Men Are Not Free Men"

Whitelands Ruskin Lecture
2014   Dinah Birch: Thinking Through the Past: John Ruskin and the Whitelands College May Festival
2015   Sara Atwood: "An enormous difference between knowledge and education': What Ruskin Can Teach Us

Occasional Lectures
2013   Clive Wilmer: 'A new road on which the world should travel': John Ruskin, 'The Nature of Gothic' and William Morris
2015   Sara Atwood. 'The earth-veil': Ruskin and Environment

www.guildofstgeorge.org.uk/shop

The Guild of St George was formally established by John Ruskin in 1878. Through the Guild, Ruskin strove to make Britain a pleasanter and happier place in which to live. His aims and aspirations for the Guild are contained in the ninety six "Letters" of his *Fors Clavigera*.

Today the Guild is a charitable Education Trust which tries to put Ruskin's ideas into practice. It owns and supports the Ruskin Collection, housed in Sheffield's Millennium Gallery, and is currently running a series of activities and events in a community heritage project, *Ruskin-in-Sheffield*, supported by the Heritage Lottery Fund. It can offer scholarships and awards across a range of subjects close to Ruskin's heart, including the practice of crafts and scholarly work in agricultural science and economics, education, industry and the social sciences.

The first of the Ruskin Triennial Exhibitions, which focused on the Environment and Sustainability, was shown at Sheffield between October 2009 and January 2010. A second exhibition, with the theme Landscape and Creativity, took place in 2013 and a third is planned on the theme of Craft, to open in the Millennium Galleries Sheffield in 2016.

The Guild is also supporting work on the sustainable development of the Wyre Forest, where it owns farmland, orchards, and 100 acres of woodland. It is regenerating old orchards and hay meadows, renovating and improving its properties, and exploring new projects and programmes of activity.

The present booklet has been prepared ahead of a planned visit by Companions to St George's Field in 2016, the 80th anniversary of the meadow being offered by Miss Knight to the Guild's care.